Bible reflections
for older people

BRF
Ministries

BRF Ministries

15 The Chambers, Vineyard
Abingdon OX14 3FE
+44 (0)1865 319700 | brf.org.uk

Bible Reading Fellowship is a charity (233280)
and company limited by guarantee (301324),
registered in England and Wales

EU Authorised Representative: Easy Access System Europe –
Mustamäe tee 50, 10621 Tallinn, Estonia, **gpsr.requests@easproject.com**

ISBN 978 1 80039 365 3
All rights reserved

This edition © Bible Reading Fellowship 2025
Cover image: ©iStock.com/maki_shmaki

Acknowledgements
Scripture quotations marked with the following abbreviations are taken from the version shown. Where no abbreviation is given, the quotation is taken from the same version as the headline reference. NIV: The Holy Bible, New International Version, Anglicised edition, copyright © 1979, 1984, 2011 by Biblica. Used by permission of Hodder & Stoughton Publishers, a Hachette UK company. All rights reserved. 'NIV' is a registered trademark of Biblica. UK trademark number 1448790. NRSV: the New Revised Standard Version Updated Edition. Copyright © 2021 National Council of Churches of Christ in the United States of America. Used by permission. All rights reserved worldwide. KJV: The Authorised Version of the Bible (The King James Bible), the rights in which are vested in the Crown, are reproduced by permission of the Crown's Patentee, Cambridge University Press. RSV: The Revised Standard Version of the Bible, copyright © 1946, 1952, 1971 by the Division of Christian Education of the National Council of the Churches of Christ in the United States of America. Used by permission. All rights reserved. NLT: The Holy Bible, New Living Translation, copyright © 1996, 2004, 2007, 2013. Used by permission of Tyndale House Publishers, Inc., Carol Stream, Illinois 60188. All rights reserved. NASB: The New American Standard Bible®, Copyright © 1960, 1971, 1977, 1995, 2020 by The Lockman Foundation. All rights reserved.

Poem 'Silently' on p. 34 used with kind permission of Andrew Rudd.

Every effort has been made to trace and contact copyright owners for material used in this resource. We apologize for any inadvertent omissions or errors, and would ask those concerned to contact us so that full acknowledgement can be made in the future.

A catalogue record for this book is available from the British Library

Printed and bound in the UK by Zenith Media NP4 0DQ

Contents

About the writers 4

From the Editor 5

Using these reflections 6

Blessings Sally Welch 7

On eagle's wings Tony Horsfall 18

The Gift of Years Debbie Thrower 29

Hidden and unseen Clare O'Driscoll 37

Questions Jesus asked David Butterfield 48

About the writers

Sally Welch is vicar of the Kington group of parishes in the diocese of Hereford. She has written numerous books for BRF Ministries and other publishers and is an expert on pilgrimage and labyrinths. She was a residentiary canon at Christ Church Cathedral, Oxford, and was formerly prayer and spirituality advisor for Oxford Diocese.

Tony Horsfall is an author, retreat leader and mentor based in Bournemouth. He is the author of *Rhythms of Grace*, *Working from a Place of Rest* and *Grief Notes*. He is married to Jilly, a counsellor, and between them they have four married children and six grandchildren. They share a passion to see people thrive in life and ministry.

Clare O'Driscoll lives with her family in West Sussex where she gives Spanish and French tuition and occasionally writes for Christian publications. She is part of the team of volunteer editors at *Magnet* magazine and also does some ghost-writing. Clare is mildly obsessed with the sea and, in between her other tasks, is working on a book reflecting on life and purpose through stories from beach cafés.

David Butterfield was born in Yorkshire. After studying music he felt the call to ordination in the Church of England. During his forty-year ministry he served at churches in Southport, the Midlands and Shropshire. His final post was based at York Minster from which he retired in 2017. He and his wife Irene now live in Ripon in North Yorkshire. They have two adult children and one grandchild.

From the Editor

Welcome!

In primary school I had a friend called Hazel. Her family had a farm at the far end of the village and an invitation to tea was an adventure: roaming fields and barns, and eating at the huge scrubbed wooden kitchen table beside a cardboard corral for skittery orphaned lambs.

Hazel won county competitions for naming the most wild flowers. I thought of her last year, walking in Scotland in May, the most glorious month for wild flowers. The woods were full of celandines, bluebells and wild garlic... and many others Hazel would have known the names of.

Bible Reflections for Older People writer Martyn Payne wrote a lovely article about his joy at discovering the names of wild flowers on summer walks with his wife. Bird's foot trefoil, traveller's joy, periwinkle, ragged robin, meadow sweet, lady's bedstraw... he recalled Jesus' words: 'Consider how the wild flowers grow. They do not labour or spin. Yet I tell you, not even Solomon in all his splendour was dressed like one of these. If that is how God clothes the grass of the field... how much more will he clothe you – you of little faith' (Luke 12:27–28, NIV).

'With these words,' wrote Martyn, 'Jesus invites us to come close to God as we come close to God's world.' Noticing the wild flowers, walking in the woods, looking out of the window or even, in our mind's eye, recalling the daisies of childhood, can be 'an opportunity to renew our hope and faith in God. The wild flowers we see can teach us eternal truths.'

Go well

Using these reflections

Perhaps you have always had a special time each day for reading the Bible and praying. But now, as you grow older, you are finding it more difficult to keep to a regular pattern or find it harder to concentrate. Or, maybe you've never done this before. Whatever your situation, these Bible reflections aim to help you take a few moments to read God's Word and pray whenever you have time or feel that would be helpful.

When to read them

You might use these Bible reflections in the morning or last thing at night, but they work at any time of day. There are 40 reflections here, grouped around four themes, by four different writers. Each one includes some verses from the Bible, a reflection to help you in your own thinking about God, and a prayer suggestion. The reflections aren't dated, so it doesn't matter if you don't want to read every day. The Bible verses are printed, but you might prefer to follow them in your own Bible.

How to read them

- **Take time** to quieten yourself, becoming aware of God's presence, asking him to speak to you through the Bible and the reflection.
- **Read** the Bible verses and the reflection:
  - What do you especially like or find helpful in these verses?
  - What might God be saying to you through this reading?
  - Is there something to pray about or thank God for?
- **Pray.** Each reflection includes a prayer suggestion. You might like to pray for yourself or take the opportunity to think about and pray for others.

Blessings

Sally Welch

As I write these reflections, I am sitting at the bedside of my father, who has been unwell for several weeks. Members of the family are taking it in turns to nurse him, but despite this, I have sat here for many hours. In the stillness of this greatly reduced world, shrunk now to just one room, I have learnt much. Surprisingly, for one who finds energy in motion, and the ultimate challenge to be contemplative prayer, this time has been one of fruitfulness.

I have drawn closer to my family, especially my father; I have cultivated new hobbies which can be carried out in a small space; I have discovered the joys of watching the same trees change from bare branches to buds then leaves as the seasons pass. The greatest gift, however, has been the opportunity for reflection and uninterrupted thought. Within this I have found and meditated upon some of the many blessings of the Christian life, communicated to us through the words of scripture and which it is my privilege to share with you now.

> Surely goodness and mercy shall follow me all the days of my life, and I shall dwell in the house of the Lord my whole life long.
> PSALM 23:6 (NRSV)

Deuteronomy 16:9–10 (NRSV)

Attitude of gratitude

You shall count seven weeks; begin to count the seven weeks from the time the sickle is first put to the standing grain. Then you shall keep the Festival of Weeks to the Lord your God, contributing a freewill offering in proportion to the blessing that you have received from the Lord your God.

The Festival of Weeks is one of three occasions when the Jewish people are instructed by God to gather and present the first fruits of the land as a thank offering for his generous provision for them. Our own tradition of harvest festivals is based on this – a time when we gather to praise the creator of the universe for all that we have been given.

Although grand celebrations and big calendar events are appropriate, thanking God for the blessings he has given us should not be an occasional event but the work of every day. Gratitude journals can be really helpful as a prompt, offering space for noting down small moments of happiness and thankfulness during the day, but simply setting aside a regular time for an appreciation of God's good works can be just as effective a reminder of all that we have been given.

■ PRAYER

All good gifts around us are sent from heaven above, then thank the Lord, O thank the Lord for all his love. (Matthias Claudius, 1782)

Ruth 2:2a, 4 (NRSV)

A working relationship

And Ruth the Moabite said to Naomi, 'Let me go to the field and glean among the ears of grain, behind someone in whose sight I may find favour'… Just then Boaz came from Bethlehem. He said to the reapers, 'The Lord be with you.' They answered, 'The Lord bless you.'

The book of Ruth is said to be the only book in the Bible where no one misbehaves! It is a short, lyrical tale of good men and women living in ways which honour God and each other, and the consequent part they play in the story of the redemption of all God's people. In this extract we see the ideal employer/employee relationship.

Boaz, coming to inspect his fields, greets his workers with respect and courtesy. In a few words he acknowledges their mutually dependent relationship and their common humanity. In return, the reapers bless him, demonstrating that blessing is not an action available only to the strong and those in power, but to all children of God.

It may not be possible for us to bless openly those we encounter in our daily lives, but we can certainly aim to 'think' or pray a blessing on them, and I know from experience this changes our own attitude towards others in a way which brings its own blessings.

■ PRAYER

God of all people, help me to see the face of Christ in those around me, and treat them accordingly. Amen

Isaiah 44:2b–4 (NRSV)

My cup will overflow

Do not fear, O Jacob my servant, Jeshurun whom I have chosen. For I will pour water on the thirsty land, and streams on the dry ground; I will pour my spirit upon your descendants, and my blessing on your offspring. They shall spring up like a green tamarisk, like willows by flowing streams.

The people of Israel have been captured and are currently languishing in exile in Babylon. Isaiah makes it clear that this is due to their own sinfulness, but God has not abandoned them. Just as he led his children out of Egypt, God will act to restore the broken and bereft to a position of wholeness and health. The glorious thing about this passage is that the promised blessing is not just given but 'poured' out upon the people, in such copious quantities that it flows like a stream, enabling them to grow and flourish in their newly restored heritage.

There are times of dryness and bitter thirst in all of our lives – times when we feel weary and unrefreshed. But when the land around us is hard and we are fearful for the future, let us put our faith in the promise of the stream of blessings which will be poured out for us and by which we will be restored to greenness once more.

■ PRAYER

Lord, I thirst. Let me drink from the living water which is your Son, Jesus Christ. Amen

Luke 1:46–49 (NRSV)

Courageous faith

And Mary said, 'My soul magnifies the Lord, and my spirit rejoices in God my Saviour, for he has looked with favour on the lowliness of his servant. Surely, from now on all generations will call me blessed, for the Mighty One has done great things for me, and holy is his name.

We know Mary is special, because she has been chosen as the God-bearer. But this response to the awesome, terrifying, world-changing task that God has given her demonstrates her truly inspiring courage as well. In the face of all the challenges that she will face, some of which she has already had to deal with, her reaction is to call herself blessed, and to place her trust wholly and completely in the Mighty One whose name is holy.

In our lives we will all be given pieces of news which will be difficult to bear; let us follow the example of Mary – believe in our cherished position as much-loved children of God and place our faith in the one who is holy. Then we might face the future with the courage and hope of Mary, mother of God: 'For all that has been; thanks. For all that will be; yes' (Dag Hammarskjöld).

■ PRAYER

Lord God, I do not know what the future holds, but I know you hold the future. Give me courage, strength and hope for all that the future will bring. Amen

Matthew 5:3–6 (NRSV)

Transforming lives

'Blessed are the poor in spirit, for theirs is the kingdom of heaven. Blessed are those who mourn, for they will be comforted. Blessed are the meek, for they will inherit the earth. Blessed are those who hunger and thirst for righteousness, for they will be filled.'

This section from the sermon on the mount is delivered to the disciples, after Jesus has moved away from the crowds. These beatitudes offer an insight into the character of Jesus, as they are lived out through his actions in the gospel.

But they go further than merely showing us who Jesus is; they show us how we can become more like him, more like us the people God designed us to be. We are called to put aside the values of the world and follow those of the kingdom of God; to walk alongside those in trouble or need; to choose to be not just changed but transformed.

We are challenged to make God the centre of our lives and are promised, in return, the blessing of a life which abides in his love.

■ PRAYER
Thanks be to thee, my Lord Jesus Christ,
for all the benefits thou hast given me,
for all the pains and insults thou hast borne for me.
O most merciful redeemer, friend and brother,
may I know thee more clearly,
love thee more dearly,
and follow thee more nearly, day by day. Amen
(Richard of Chichester)

Mark 10:14–16 (NRSV)

Moments of tenderness

But when Jesus saw this, he was indignant and said to them, 'Let the little children come to me; do not stop them; for it is to such as these that the kingdom of God belongs. Truly I tell you, whoever does not receive the kingdom of God as a little child will never enter it.' And he took them up in his arms, laid his hands on them, and blessed them.

For the past 15 months I have shared a house which is slightly too small for the number of people who live in it. Among these have been three very young children, who have by turns delighted, amazed, amused and totally exhausted me.

I have had to draw upon reservoirs of patience I didn't know I had, as well as learn to set aside my own preferences in terms of television programmes, meal choices and free-time activities, but have been rewarded with the experience of observing the world through the eyes of a small child, in all its glory and mystery. Jesus instructs us to greet God's world and all who dwell in it with the same enthusiasm, grace and generosity. Then we will know the same blessings of wonder, welcome and joy in our turn.

■ **PRAYER**

He gave us eyes to see them,
and lips that we might tell
how great is God Almighty,
who has made all things well. Amen
(Cecil Frances Alexander, 1848)

John 20:27–29 (NRSV)

Blessed believers

Then he said to Thomas, 'Put your finger here and see my hands. Reach out your hand and put it in my side. Do not doubt but believe.' Thomas answered him, 'My Lord and my God!' Jesus said to him, 'Have you believed because you have seen me? Blessed are those who have not seen and yet have come to believe.'

Christianity has been woven into the fabric of my life since birth – at times, admittedly, it has not been a very vivid or strong thread, but it has never disappeared entirely. I don't think, however, that this means I have taken my faith for granted.

Rather, I have made a deliberate choice always to view the world through the lens of a belief in the life, death and resurrection of Christ, with its consequential action of the redemption of the world. Sometimes that choice has been easy, but at difficult, stressful or challenging times, I have had to be very intentional about that choice, almost forcing myself to nurture and protect my belief and not pick up instead the distorting lens of a cruel, indifferent world with no hope of eternity. This prayer is for all believers with more than a bit of Thomas in them.

■ **PRAYER**

'Jesus said unto him, If thou canst believe, all things are possible to him that believeth. And straightway the father of the child cried out, and said with tears, Lord, I believe; help thou mine unbelief' (Mark 9:23–24, KJV).

1 Peter 3:8–9 (NRSV)

Children of God

Finally, all of you, have unity of spirit, sympathy, love for one another, a tender heart, and a humble mind. Do not repay evil for evil or abuse for abuse; but, on the contrary, repay with a blessing. It is for this that you were called – that you might inherit a blessing.

I recently led a pilgrimage along the new St Frideswide's Way, which follows the Thames Path from Oxford to Reading. Along the way we reflected on the theme of 'calling' – that of the saints who first brought Christianity to this part of the country, and of our own as a 'royal priesthood' whose purpose is to 'proclaim the excellence of [God]' (1 Peter 2:9).

This sounds very daunting – far gentler is Peter's exhortation to us all simply to repay whatever is given to us with a blessing. I am reminded of the quote by Mother Teresa: 'If you want to change the world, go home and love your family.' Perhaps we can extend this simply to loving everyone with whom we engage, passing on the blessings we have received so that others can be blessed in turn.

■ PRAYER

Make me a blessing, make me a blessing.
Out of my life may Jesus shine;
make me a blessing, O Saviour, I pray.
Make me a blessing to someone today. Amen
(Ira B. Wilson, 1909)

James 1:12–14 (NRSV)

The blame game

Blessed is anyone who endures temptation. Such a one has stood the test and will receive the crown of life that the Lord has promised to those who love him. No one, when tempted, should say, 'I am being tempted by God'; for God cannot be tempted by evil and he himself tempts no one. But one is tempted by one's own desire, being lured and enticed by it.

In among all the gentleness and love, it is quite bracing to encounter this message about blessing. It is so easy, is it not, to pass the blame for our shortcomings on to another. Perhaps this stems from early experiences of being blamed for something we did not do, or simply from finding admonition for wrongdoing uncomfortable.

So much more comfortable to make heroes of ourselves – if God is tempting us, no wonder we cannot withstand it. But James is quite definite here – it is clearly on us to take responsibility for our waywardness. But just as the blame is ours when we fail, so is the reward when we successfully resist wrongdoing.

And we remember that every time we fail (for all do fail), forgiveness awaits in the outstretched hand of God, leading us back to the paths of righteousness once more.

■ PRAYER
Lord God, help me to see beyond the cheap lure of worldly attractions to the glorious crown of life which waits beyond. Amen

Psalm 113:2–4 (NRSV)

The heart's choice

Blessed be the name of the Lord from this time on and forevermore. From the rising of the sun to its setting the name of the Lord is to be praised. The Lord is high above all nations, and his glory above the heavens.

And so we end where we began, praising God for all he has done for us, walking forward into the future confident in the goodness of his loving purposes, secure in the knowledge that we are his people and he is our God.

Through good times and bad, periods of intense activity and seasons of silent stillness, we do not walk alone along the paths of life but in the company of our guide and destination, Jesus Christ himself.

And as we journey, we count our blessings, pour out blessings on others and worship the source of all goodness and blessing, returning each good gift to its origin through joyful praise of its creator. 'Bless the Lord, O my soul, and all that is within me, bless his holy name' (Psalm 103:1).

■ PRAYER

The Lord bless you and keep you; the Lord make his face to shine upon you and be gracious to you; the Lord lift up his countenance upon you and give you peace (Numbers 6:24–26).

On eagle's wings

Tony Horsfall

I don't think I'm alone in finding chapter 40 of the book of Isaiah one of the most inspiring chapters in the Bible, and for the next few days I'm going to focus in some detail on the last few verses of the chapter, Isaiah 40:25–31.

The prophecy of Isaiah falls into two sections. In chapters 1—39 we see Israel's sin and refusal to repent, which leads to them being taken into exile in Babylon. Then, in chapters 40—66 the prophet announces the good news that God will one day bring them back to the promised land and restore his blessing to a now obedient people.

Chapter 40, with its great message of comfort for God's people, is therefore a turning point in the whole book, and well-known because it features in Handel's *Messiah*. Another theme which emerges here is the greatness of God as creator of the universe and Lord of the nations.

The relevance of the verses on which we will reflect is that this awesome God can strengthen us in our weakness and enable us to cope with the challenges of life. We all feel tired and weary at times and wonder if we can carry on. Isaiah assures us that with God's power we most certainly can.

Isaiah 40:26 (NIV)

The God of power and might

Lift up your eyes and look to the heavens: who created all these? He who brings out the starry host one by one and calls forth each of them by name. Because of his great power and mighty strength, not one of them is missing.

Can you think of times when you've seen the night sky when it is really dark and clear? If so, you will have been amazed at the myriad of stars that can be seen by the naked eye. With a telescope, and the help of an astronomer, you may be able to identify planets, constellations and whole galaxies. Truly awe-inspiring.

Isaiah presents us with a majestic view of God, who sustains and holds the whole universe in place. In particular, he delights that as the powerful creator of the universe, God's strength is made available to us in our weakness. He holds us by his mighty power, just as he holds the stars. We are safe and secure in the grip of his love.

If today you're feeling especially weak and vulnerable, remember that the creator God is aware of you, cares for you and has a loving hold on your life.

■ PRAYER

Lord, you know my circumstances. I choose to rest in the knowledge that you are watching over me every moment of every day. You keep the universe going, and you can keep me going too. Amen

Isaiah 40:27 (NIV)

Abandoned by God?

Why do you complain, Jacob? Why do you say, Israel, 'My way is hidden from the Lord; my cause is disregarded by my God'?

As Isaiah seeks to comfort the people of Israel, he is aware that God knows everything about them, even what they are thinking. Depending on how we look at it, that may be either comforting or deeply disturbing. Either way, nothing is hidden from God.

Most British people like me find it difficult to complain openly. It is a national characteristic that we prefer to give the impression that all is well when it is not. Even if on the inside we are seething with anger, we smile politely, say nothing and refuse to disclose our true feelings.

We may deceive others, but we can never fool God. He knows what we are feeling and thinking, even when we are angry with him. Who hasn't occasionally questioned God's apparent unresponsiveness to their prayers? Sometimes he seems unaware of our 'ways' (what is happening to us) and indifferent to our 'cause' (the things that are important to us).

The fact that God knows what is going on inside us reminds us that he is aware of our concerns and has not abandoned us. His help will come in his time, and in his way.

■ **PRAYER**

Lord, forgive me when I grumble and complain. Help me to trust you, and to patiently wait for you to act. Amen

Isaiah 40:28 (NIV)

God who never grows tired

Do you not know? Have you not heard? The Lord is the everlasting God, the Creator of the ends of the earth. He will not grow tired or weary, and his understanding no one can fathom.

It's a common experience to find as we grow older that we have less energy. Taking an afternoon nap is quite permissible, and not a sign of laziness. Never be afraid to have a siesta!

Likewise, a human tendency, especially in later life, is to grow weary: to lose our enthusiasm for certain commitments and tasks. The burden of responsibility can weigh more heavily upon us, and it is right and proper to shed a few responsibilities, lest we become overwhelmed.

God, however, is the everlasting God, the creator, and he never grows tired or weary. He can continue to sustain the universe and care for its people without needing a rest or growing weary with the responsibility.

He is so much greater than we are. We are weak and frail human beings, limited in our understanding. Try as we might, we cannot always fathom what God is doing, or not doing. His ways and his thoughts are so much higher than ours, so rather than complain we must learn to trust him, believing that he is good, wise and kind in all he does.

■ PRAYER

Lord, help me to rest in your greatness, and not judge you by my own finite understanding. Amen

Isaiah 40:29 (NIV)

Strength for the weary

He gives strength to the weary and increases the power of the weak.

As I grow older, I find I am not as strong as I used to be, and that can be disconcerting. I cannot run like I used to or lift heavy boxes like before. I have less stamina and want to go to bed earlier, especially in the winter. I'm glad when someone offers me a seat on the bus. Growing old is not always easy, especially in a society that values physical fitness and strength so highly.

Accepting the inevitable changes that come with ageing is part of finding contentment, but it doesn't mean we should sit back and give up. With God's help we can often do more than we imagine.

God *gives* strength to the weary. He shares his own life and energy with us as a gift.

God *increases* the strength we have. As with the loaves and fishes, he can make a little go a long way, and if we give what strength we have to God, we may be surprised by what we can still achieve.

■ PRAYER
Whatever physical challenges you face today, ask for God's strength in your weakness.

Isaiah 40:30 (NIV)

Young people grow weary too

Even youths grow tired and weary, and young men stumble and fall.

We expect that older people will grow tired and weary, but young people? Aren't they supposed to have boundless energy, be full of ambition and enjoying the prime of life? The Bible is so realistic and full of understanding of the human condition. It speaks to all generations, every culture and period of history. Not surprisingly, it has something to say to younger people in the 21st century.

If you have children, and perhaps grandchildren, you will be acutely aware that the world is now a very different place from the one we grew up in. Young people face challenges we never did, in particular the impact of social media.

The development of the internet and advances in mobile technology mean younger people are in constant touch with work, family and friends, and world events. More worryingly, they're exposed to the darker corners of the internet at an ever younger age. Everyone wants their attention and their 'clicks', and there is little opportunity to slow down and rest. Trying to meet so many expectations is exhausting. No wonder young people today are often anxious, fidgety and sleep deprived. They need God's help and our prayers.

■ PRAYER

Lord, I pray for young people [or name someone known to you] to encounter you in a life-changing way, and to experience the rest that you alone can give. Amen

Isaiah 40:31a (NIV)

Hope in the Lord

But those who hope in the Lord will renew their strength.

When I was facing a major operation, a friend who had been through the same surgery said to me, 'Tony, the people who cope best are those who maintain a positive mental attitude and who expect to get well.' I thought it was good advice and I worked hard at maintaining a positive outlook and believing there would be a good outcome, which, thankfully, there was.

When we have a personal faith, and live in a relationship with Jesus, it is easier to think positively rather than to sink into the mire of imagining the worst. Yet it is still a battle and requires us to exercise faith – to believe that God is with us and will bring us through.

I believe that is what is meant by the expression 'hope in the Lord'. Hope has been defined as 'a confident expectation of good to come', but this is not simply positive thinking, mind over matter or 'hoping for the best'. Christian hope has a focus, and the focus is God. We hope in the Lord. We trust in him. That is what makes the difference.

■ PRAYER

Lord, today I turn my eyes upon you, the creator of the universe. I know that you love me, and that your power is at work within me. Strengthen me and grant me the grace to cope – in hope – with the challenges I face. Amen

Isaiah 40:31a (RSV)

Waiting for God

But they who wait for the Lord shall renew their strength.

Yes, it is the same verse as yesterday, but in a different translation. The Revised Standard Version translation brings out another helpful understanding of how we receive God's strength when we are under pressure. We do so by *waiting for the Lord*.

Here is an expression commonly found in the Bible, but not always easy to understand. Simply put, it means that we relate best to God through patience and trust. Receiving God's strength is a process, and it may well take time.

In a day of instant responses, we sometimes assume that God's promises will come to pass immediately and we may feel impatient if there is any delay. But waiting for God means waiting for him to act, when he chooses and in his time frame.

Waiting for God also requires that we trust God. In the interval between the promise being given and its fulfilment, we may be tempted to doubt God, or to feel as Israel did, abandoned by him (v. 27). Yet trust is our faith response to the knowledge that God is good and totally reliable. Hoping in God, and waiting for him to act, are therefore like two sides of the same coin.

■ PRAYER

Lord, I do find waiting difficult. Help me to be patient and more trusting of you. Amen.

Isaiah 40:31a (NIV)

They will soar

They will soar on wings like eagles; they will run and not grow weary, they will walk and not be faint.

The life of being sustained by God is now described by the prophet in three beautiful word pictures, and using three simple but strong verbs. Those who depend on God will soar, they will run and they will walk.

The first picture shows that Isaiah was in tune with the natural world for he draws our attention to the most magnificent of all birds, the eagle, and in particular, the way it flies. It doesn't flap like smaller birds, anxiously trying to stay airborne. Rather it opens out its giant wings, catches the thermal current and then allows itself to be carried upwards into the sky, without effort or striving. There it can circle for long periods, held aloft by the current, flying without expending energy at all. It is soaring.

The analogy is clear. When we depend on God, and take time to be in his presence, the Holy Spirit will carry us along. We need simply to open ourselves to his presence and trust him to empower us. He will uphold us.

■ **PRAYER**

Reflect on this promise from God: 'Even to your old age and grey hairs I am he, I am he who will sustain you. I have made you and I will carry you; I will sustain you and I will rescue you' (Isaiah 46:4). Amen

Isaiah 40:31b (NIV)

They will run

They will soar on wings like eagles; they will run and not grow weary, they will walk and not be faint.

As we read in the last reflection, Isaiah describes the life of being sustained by God in three beautiful pictures, using three simple but strong verbs. Those who depend on God will soar, they will run and they will walk.

I had thought my running days were over until a couple of years ago when my wife encouraged me to join her on the Saturday morning Park Run – not to run, but to walk around the course. I did, and enjoyed it, so have continued to take part. Sometimes I even jog sections of the course.

Isaiah uses the action of running as a metaphor for Christian service, similar to the way it is so often used in the New Testament. 'Let us run with perseverance the race marked out for us,' writes the author of the letter to the Hebrews (12:1).

As we learn to depend ever more fully on God, we can serve without becoming exhausted. Each of us has our own path to follow, and we can finish our race because God will strengthen us every step of the way.

■ **PRAYER**

Lord, I take a moment right now to wait on you. In the quiet I receive your strength for all that you have given me to do and all that lies before me today. Amen

Isaiah 40:b (NIV)

They will walk

They will soar on wings like eagles; they will run and not grow weary, they will walk and not be faint.

Isaiah's threefold description of the life of being sustained by God finishes with the promise that we will walk and not faint. Here we have a metaphor of the Christian life as a journey of making steady progress, day by day. It is not spectacular, but it is consistent. It speaks not about service but about how we live out our faith, applying the wisdom of God to every aspect of our daily lives.

Enoch was the first person in the Bible to be described as someone who walked with God (Genesis 5:21–24). It is a lovely picture, suggesting two friends going for a stroll together and enjoying each other's company. Perhaps you can imagine your life with God in that beautiful way. It also says that Enoch walked faithfully with God until the end of his life, enjoying God's presence and consistently walking in his ways.

That is certainly something to which I aspire. It is what someone called 'a long obedience in the same direction', and it is a worthy goal for any Christian.

■ PRAYER

Lord, I too aspire to walk with you, and to do so all the days of my life. Your companionship means so much to me. I trust you never to leave me or forsake me. Amen

The Gift of Years

Debbie Thrower is the founder of BRF Ministries' Anna Chaplaincy for Older People. She retired in late 2023 and is now a vice president of BRF Ministries.

Visit **annachaplaincy.org.uk** to find out more.

Debbie writes...

Welcome!

It's a truism that you never forget a kindness. Think back to your teachers or to old friends or family in the past, and the chances are you can remember specific moments of how kind they were to you.

Jesus was a good listener. So it's no suprise that one of the key foundations of Anna Chaplaincy is good listening, a kindness in itself. He asked the sort of questions which elicited interesting and telling replies, chief among them, 'What do you want me to do for you?' How practical, how kind. I'm looking forward to reflecting, along with David Butterfield, on the variety of questions Jesus asked of the people he met and cared about so much.

Other writers in this issue have chosen diverse, rewarding topics: Sally Welch asks what it is to bless, and be blessed? And Clare O'Driscoll asks what do we hide – from others, from God – and what is hidden from us?

Tony Horsfall focuses on a handful of verses from Isaiah, but they speak of both the awesome power of our creator God and the comfort and strength he gives to his people.

Enjoy this feast for the imagination, intended to deepen our appreciation of life in all its richness.

With best wishes

Journey to contentment

We're delighted to welcome Sally Welch to *Bible Reflections for Older People* and wish her well as she settles into her new role as vicar of the Kington group of parishes in the diocese of Hereford, right on the Offa's Dyke long distance trail. Sally is an expert on pilgrimage and journeying, and we celebrate her wisdom and experience in this extract from her book *Journey to Contentment: Pilgrimage principles for everyday life* (BRF Ministries, 2020). The book begins and ends with the same verses: Paul's well-known words to the Christians in Philippi:

> For I have learned to be content whatever the circumstances. I know what it is to be in need, and I know what it is to have plenty. I have learned the secret of being content in any and every situation, whether well fed or hungry, whether living in plenty or in want. I can do all this through him who gives me strength.
> PHILIPPIANS 4:11–13 (NIV)

It seems to me that the process of learning becomes harder as we grow older – we are more secure with what we do know and perhaps less willing to embark on the adventure of the unknown, with its promise of uncertainty. Skilled at some things, we are reluctant to start right back at the beginning again, experiencing once more those first faltering steps on the way to gaining a new accomplishment.

So it is not surprising that we read those three words of Paul with some trepidation: 'I have learned.' We know that what follows is the result of effort, of hard work, of failures as well as successes, of slow progress as well as sudden inspiration. But we also know that what is being shared with us is of great value, because Paul considered it worth the effort: 'I have learned to be content with whatever I have.'

Contentment is not a secret, but it is a mystery. The state of contentment is achieved with grace, but it is not given as a gift – it is learned, and the lessons can be hard work. Contentment is not something which can be assumed or faked, and we quickly spot those who merely seem to have achieved it.

The glib assertions that a person 'doesn't need much to be content' or is 'happy with only a little' are betrayed by an anxious restlessness or a half hidden yearning.

They show, too, a misunderstanding of the nature of contentment – it is not merely a willingness to be happy with what one has been given, however meagre that amount is. Contentment is a profound spiritual act, a way of living and being which combines an acceptance of all that God provides with a desire to move ever deeper into relationship with the creator. Contentment is born of an attitude of trust in the purposes of God for each one of us and a willingness to step out boldly into the unknown for the sake of his kingdom.

We must begin our journey to contentment with an attitude of humility, willing to learn – however challenging that act of learning will be. We must be prepared to work hard and suffer setbacks, but with the knowledge that such setbacks are not the end of the journey, only obstacles along the way, and that the prize is truly worth the effort

Spend some time reflecting on the things you have learned over your life. Try to make a list of them. It might help to divide the list into different areas – things you have learned about the way other people behave, skills you have acquired, experiences you have had which have led to wisdom or insight. Choose one or two, and try to remember what it felt like to be a beginner, just setting out on the path to learning. Remember the successes and the setbacks, and the feelings that each brought. Try to recapture that attitude of determination and excitement which heralds the start of a new project – and put it towards this new venture of learning contentment.

You would not know that the writer of Philippians was in prison? You would not know that he had suffered all sorts of punishments and indignities, nor that he would eventually be executed for his faith.

This passage is filled with joy, hope and a sense that whatever the future holds, the writer will be equal to it, because his certainty is centred not within himself, but in God, who holds his future in love.

This hope is not an empty one, but one based on previous experience, on the testimony of others and on a faith lived out in the most extreme circumstances. But it is also the hope born of a choice made deliberately by the writer, Paul, himself. He could have chosen to be bitter, to write in despairing terms about all the hardships that had happened to him and about the bleakness of the future that he and the people of Philippi undoubtedly faced.

But he doesn't – he focuses on the positive points, and his letter is alive with his determination to make the most of the gifts that have been given to him and to use them in service to God. 'I have learned the secret,' he writes, and we too are learning that secret – which is to be content with whatever befalls us, because we trust that God is in charge of the outcome. We are learning the secret of being grateful for all that we have been given, for living in grateful expectation of future grace. We are learning that, although we may not always be able to decide what will happen to us, we can all determine how we will respond to that which has happened – and that response must be rooted and grounded in love.

'I can do all things,' writes the prisoner, the shipwrecked one, the beaten, starved and tortured one. 'I can do all things' because I live not in my own strength but in the strength of the one who created me. 'I can do all things' because life itself is a gift, not a right; a privilege, not a debt owed to me. 'I can do all things' because the weaker and more flawed I am, the more the grace of God shines through me; the less confident I am in my own strength, the more the strength of God sustains me. 'I can do all things… through him who strengthens me.'

Conversations with wonder

The poet **Andrew Rudd's** work first appeared in *Bible Reflections for Older People* in the September–December 2018 issue. Three years later, a second poem and an interview appeared. At that time Andrew was 'inching towards retirement' from paid work. He was also reflecting on the impact that lockdown had had on his writing

Although it wasn't a good time for conventional writing, something new emerged:

'There was another kind of writing which I did during lockdown,' he told us, 'which was when I was out walking, talking into my phone and then transcribing it when I came back. If I wrote any poetry over that time, it came out of walking and talking.'

The fruit of that walking and talking emerged in a quietly stunning collection of 'small noticings, gifts of attention, conversations with wonder,' named Hob Hey, after the wooded valley in Cheshire where Andrew did most of his lockdown walking.

Originally self-published for friends and family, what began as Hob Hey has now been developed into a bigger, longer, but equally enchanting book called *The Quiet Path: Contemplative practices for daily life* (SCM Canterbury, 2024). As one reviewer writes:

'Through the author's poetry, attention and most of all his quiet humble walking, we walk with him into the place of dwelling, of prayer, of the heart…'

In keeping with our own themes of walking and pilgrimage, whether outside in the woods or in our minds eye, we're delighted to include another of Andrew's poems, from Hob Hey.

Silently

*I practiced walking
ever more silently
down the lane
into the wood*

*not a scuffle or shoe
not a breaking twig*

*on the pathways
I had walked for so long
I became a ghost
invisible
a shadow*

*at my passing you might feel
the air move slightly
to one side
or a bird suddenly up
from the hedge*

*no images
no metaphors
I can only speak of the unseen world
there's a skylark singing
every note infinite*

Used with kind permission of Andrew Rudd.

Hob Hey (£7.00 inc p&p) is available from the author. If you would like to contact him please email **enquiries@brf.org.uk** and we'll forward your message.

Clouds: a meditation by Joanna Collicutt

There is more to life than meets the eye; things are what they seem but also more than they seem. We talk of the need to 'see through', to 'see another side', to 'see for myself'. Living in the light of heaven is an acknowledgement that there is more to life than we yet know – that there is something beyond – perhaps in the future (time) or over the horizon (space) or again behind or beneath 'the foreground of existence'.

The images of catching a glimpse through a blowing curtain, peering through a clear spot on a steamed-up window, squinting through a chink in a door, 'seeing through a glass darkly', all capture this well. But perhaps above all it is clouds that convey it best – clouds in their infinite variety of colour, form and scale, beautiful and ever-changing, veiling in layer upon layer that which lies beyond, parting unbidden to reveal the wide blue yonder or pierced by rays of sunlight that promise so much. The clouds are literally heavenly:

> The heavens are telling the glory of God, and the firmament proclaims his handiwork. Day to day pours forth speech, and night to night declares knowledge. There is no speech, nor are there words; their voice is not heard; yet their voice goes out through all the earth and their words to the end of the world.
> PSALM 19:1–4 (NRSV)

Our desire to see beyond the veil – for the clouds to part – is not simple curiosity about the nature of things. It is a yearning to 'see face to face', to encounter fully one who knows and loves us better than anyone else. A hospital chaplain once put it this way:

> We say God and life and death are mysteries… not because they are unknowable, but because there is so much to know that you can never know the depths of it; there is always more you can learn… The more you learn, the more you want to know…

I suppose it's faith. Belief that there is something deeply good in the mysterious heart of the infinitely knowable other.

We will only see this clearly the other side of the grave. Yet it begins now, and if we keep our eyes open we may experience little foretastes when, as for Jesus, the clouds part and love shines through:

> And when Jesus had been baptised, just as he came up from the water, suddenly the heavens were opened to him and he saw the God's Spirit descending like a dove and alighting on him. And a voice from the heavens said, 'This is my Son, the Beloved, with whom I am well pleased.'
> MATTHEW 3:16–17 (NRSV)

Joanna's meditation is taken from *Death & Life: A church's guide to exploring mortality* published by BRF Ministries in the spring of 2024. *Death & Life* is a rich, research-based resource for churches to help people reflect on death and mortality as part of the process of healthy ageing. As a society we're not good at talking about death but there's strong evidence to show that people of all ages welcome opportunities to do so.

As lead author Joanna writes: 'Reflecting on our own death can enable us to live more fully in the here and now because the issues that come into sharp focus as death approaches turn out to be the same issues that are important in living life well.' The writers have identified six themes that encapsulate these important issues: loving, letting go, seeing, growing, belonging and hoping. Joanna's meditation is taken from the section on 'Seeing'.

To find out more about *Death & Life: A church's guide to exploring mortality* (£24.99) and the set of reflection cards created to accompany the course, please go to **brfonline.org.uk/death-life**.

Hidden and unseen

Clare O'Driscoll

I'd been rumbled. My heart beat wildly as I watched my mother poking around behind the landing cupboard. For some time now I'd been sacrificially squirreling away chunks of leftover fish fingers to feed to our cat Tuppence on the quiet, but I may have forgotten a few. Now, a slightly dubious smell had given them away. Hiding things can backfire.

Of course, my hidden fish fingers were simply the kind-hearted, if misguided, gesture of a child, but there are other kinds of hiding that cause pain and hold us back from the freedom God gives.

Sometimes truth can be hidden. And often we hide too, worried that if people really knew us, they would not like what they see. Sadly, God can also become hidden from us by the layers of safety nets we wrap ourselves in.

So, in this series, we look at the things we hide and those which are hidden. Some are hidden for admirable reasons – the quiet unseen work that keeps communities going or the seeking of deep truths. Others, however, are hidden by our distractions and mistaken perspectives, and there perhaps we need to let God draw us out into his all-seeing light.

Jeremiah 29:13–14a (NIV)

Lost in the mess

'You will seek me and find me when you seek me with all your heart. I will be found by you,' declares the Lord.

Somewhere, I have a rectangular yellow card, smaller than a playing card. On it are the simple words, 'Source of all'. I chose it during a prayer activity on a youth weekend over 25 years ago and have never thrown it away.

I find it when I'm clearing out a bits-and-pieces drawer on a rainy Saturday and decide to keep it despite it being a little dog-eared. Then, months later, rummaging for lost keys, there it is again, buried so deep under papers it seems less important than it actually is.

Whenever I find it, there's a rush of warmth as I remember the truth in those words. God really is my 'source of all'. I keep it in sight for a while, have it as a focus. But inevitably it gets 'put away' at some point and forgotten about again.

Such knowledge, such truths, can get buried under the detritus of daily life. When we rediscover them, something deep within us echoes their importance. They are still meaningful. Today, perhaps we can ask ourselves what truths we have lost sight of in the busyness and mess of life.

■ PRAYER

Help us, Father, to make a conscious choice to look for your truths. Give us clarity when other distractions hide them from our hearts. Amen

Hebrews 11:1 (NIV)

A smudge of mist

Now faith is confidence in what we hope for and assurance about what we do not see.

I tilt my head sideways, gazing out of the passenger window as the car forges on. The sky is smudged with grey, but streaks of light burst through and, in the distance, a shadow runs along the horizon, so hidden in mist that you could be forgiven for thinking it's part of the cloud formation.

But I know otherwise.

It is a line of hills as real and solid as the ground we drive on. I know, because I saw them before the mist fell. I can hold on to that memory of knowing and have complete confidence in what they really are. Because it has already been shown to me.

Sometimes God, or our faith, seems lost in a mist to us, hidden. Perhaps troubles or the vast inequalities in the world have made everything harder to hold on to. We wonder if we imagined it all. But as we tilt our heads and remember, we know God is there, real as the hills. He is not a smudge of mist, but solid ground. We can hold on to that memory of knowing, even when foggy, difficult times try to hide the truth from us.

■ **PRAYER**

Father God, thank you for your real presence with us. When things become foggy, help us to remember all that you have done and to find our place of trust in you. Amen

Matthew 7:25a (NIV)

Hidden foundations

It did not fall, because it had its foundation on the rock.

I stared out of the window at the workmen labouring on the scrap of land next door. My six-year-old mind couldn't wrap itself around what was going on. 'They're not building a house!' I called out indignantly. 'They're just digging lots of ditches!' As rain inevitably fell, those ditches filled with mud and it became a swampy quagmire. It looked like the opposite of building, the opposite of what they were supposed to be doing; but then we rarely see what back-breaking preparations go into the finished work of others.

Laying foundations can feel slow and painful. There's nothing fun or attractive about this phase in a building but it is crucial. Similarly, when we set out to do something new – a project, learning a skill, pursuing a dream or mending a relationship, God calls us to take the time to prepare with slow foundations of prayer and wisdom.

When we rush ahead, wanting everything to come quickly, we can find we've built something with no firm structure. It collapses like a house on sand. So, while this slow building of foundations may feel like going backwards, doing the opposite of what we set out to do, it is in this hidden behind-the-scenes work that God strengthens us.

■ PRAYER

Father God, help me to build slowly, taking time to lay foundations for new pursuits with prayer and consideration, knowing that lasting change is always built on the rock of your wisdom. Amen

Matthew 6:6 (NIV)

Unseen roots

But when you pray, go into your room, close the door and pray to your Father, who is unseen. Then your Father, who sees what is done in secret, will reward you.

Recently I became fascinated by the way trees communicate, both with one another and with different parts of the natural world. Hidden deep within the rich earth, there's a symbiotic relationship going on as tiny root hairs reach out to each other like old friends, sharing resources and warning of dangers.

Roots are the genesis of a plant, where life comes from. Of course, we see the outer ones, strong and sturdy above the ground, but it is actually the tiny hidden filaments that are busy making connections via fungal networks, doing unseen good. These hidden roots are like all those invisible acts of community: feeding the hungry and sharing God's love. So much true kindness, not to mention prayer, is done in secret, in the hidden places, unseen.

It can be hard to work tirelessly, unnoticed, but we are never unseen by God, who uses those hidden acts of love to bring connection and belonging within the church, all the filaments connecting. The things that seem invisible or even pointless are seen and valued by our heavenly Father who knows all that is done in secret.

■ PRAYER

Thank you, Creator God, for those who work behind the scenes. Whenever we feel our contribution is pointless or unseen, remind us that every small filament is used for your glory. Amen

Matthew 21:42 (NIV)

Hidden beauty

Jesus said to them: 'Have you never read in the Scriptures: "The stone the builders rejected has become the cornerstone; the Lord has done this, and it is marvellous in our eyes."'

We felt a little smug. We'd found the nicest little in-between cove. Not exactly abandoned but certainly a bit forgotten by the crowds. Most people flocked to the town's two main beaches with their exquisite stretches of white sand and endless ribbon-like waves. In comparison, this small sandy bay scattered with rocks might seem an also-ran, not the first place people think of. In the end, however, it is often these quiet forgotten corners that become the most loved and valued of all.

Jesus understood how it felt to be out of favour. He was rejected and despised by the established hierarchies of his time. In turn, he always looked for those on the margins of society and saw their worth. And in his loving gaze, their hidden lives and gifts blossomed into fullness.

So, when we feel like that tiny cove, the less impressive one, perhaps a little forgotten by the world, Jesus sets his loving gaze on us, reminds us that in his eyes we have tremendous value. And we too can look for others on the margins, valuing them as Jesus did, showing them they are marvellous in his eyes.

■ **PRAYER**

Jesus, thank you that you never overlook us and we are never unseen by you. Let all our hidden gifts blossom into fullness in your loving gaze. Amen

1 Corinthians 2:9b (NLT)

Better things

'No eye has seen, no ear has heard, and no mind has imagined what God has prepared for those who love him.'

When we first adopted our rescue pup I would walk her to the local park. On the way, we often found ourselves stuck on a scrubby patch of roadside grass. She would dig her heels in, refusing to budge.

She seemed to forget that just yards further on was a lush green park with tall trees to weave around, wide open spaces, rolling lawns where she could lollop crazily with other dogs, a pond full of ducks to gaze at longingly and plentiful squirrel-chasing opportunities, albeit in vain. Yet she was stuck there, stubbornly thinking this was as good as it gets. Did she not remember?

And do we not remember? Because we too can easily get stuck on a scrap of tatty grass that holds some passing curiosity for us. We forget God's past gifts. We forget there is something unseen and far more beautiful ahead. We become blind to truth and to what God has planned for us when we focus on our own small interests, our little patch of scrubland. But our merciful God draws us onwards, whispering reminders of all the good he wants for us.

■ PRAYER

Thank you, Father God, for the depth and richness of life you offer us. Help us never to stubbornly dig our heels into our own ideas of what is important, missing what you have in store. Amen

Daniel 2:22 (NIV)

Turning aside

He reveals deep and hidden things; he knows what lies in darkness, and light dwells with him.

The guide shrugged apologetically as we climbed off the dinghy. To be honest, we were delighted with all we'd seen – seals, basking sharks and scores of smiling dolphins, gambolling within touching distance. I'd had no expectations of seeing the whale he'd desperately hoped for. It just seemed so unlikely.

That evening as my sister-in-law scrolled through her pictures from the day, her eyes widened. She sent the zoomed-in photo to the guide, and you could almost hear the groan of disappointment in his reply. 'Yes, the unmistakeable tail-flip of a humpback whale.'

While we were crazily snapping the same photos over and over, happy with what we had, she had turned the other way and seen the 'impossible'.

Sometimes that's all it takes. Sometimes God asks us to turn aside for a moment to see hidden things he wants to reveal, to trust him to lead us into something astonishing. It can be easy to follow others as they point the way ahead, but maybe that's not the right way for us. We need to look to someone else. We strain our eyes in search of truth but forget that God sees through the murky waters. He knows our way better than we do. Trust him.

■ **PRAYER**

Thank you, God, that you reveal deep and hidden things to us. Help us to be ready to turn aside and find the unexpected. Amen

Psalm 139:11–12 (NIV)

In the darkness

If I say, 'Surely the darkness will hide me and the light become night around me,' even the darkness will not be dark to you; the night will shine like the day, for darkness is as light to you.

My husband grew up on a farm in south-west Ireland. When we visit family there, I'm struck by the soft velvety darkness that covers us as night falls in layers. There is a strange sense of peace, how it hides so much, yet allows us to see the sherbety dusting of stars with sharp clarity.

Darkness is usually seen as something to fear, but sometimes it holds comfort. We need it for rest and to give rhythm to our days. And sometimes, in the darkness, we see light with greater clarity.

When we've messed up and worry what God or others might think of us, it is tempting to hide our wrongs, to curl up in the gloaming, hoping we won't be seen. But God has night vision and is never limited by the dark. His light blazes through all those shady places, banishing shame from our lives. The darkness is not a place to hide, simply a place where God's light shines with a brighter clarity. And, little by little, like a father answering the cry of a child in the night, he draws us back to his dazzling light.

■ PRAYER

Thank you, Father, that you work within the darkness. Help us to always look for your light. Amen

Psalm 32:7 (NIV)

Hiding place

You are my hiding-place; you will protect me from trouble and surround me with songs of deliverance.

Fraught with insomnia two nights before my father's funeral I looked to God for refuge. Things felt bleak, but a song was on repeat in my head. It was one of Dad's poems which a friend of his had set to music and sent to me. Feeling desperate and clinging on to the melody, I took a deep breath and went to find the words in Dad's poetry pamphlet. Reading it brought the beginnings of peace. Then, my eyes flicked across to the poem on the facing page.

At first, I didn't realise what it was about. At first it didn't seem as tidy a poem as the other one. However, as I read on, I realised I was reading a poem my father had written, maybe ten years earlier… about insomnia. The words were exactly what I needed in that moment, as was the feeling of being held and protected by God.

In times of trouble, we have a choice. We can hide *from* God or we can hide *in* God. And that one word makes all the difference. Because when we hide in God, we find songs of deliverance. Songs that lead us forward, through the pain. Songs that free us.

■ **PRAYER**

Father God, thank you for your tender care for us. Thank you that when times are hard, we can hide in you, safe under your wings. Amen

Matthew 28:20b (NIV)

Voice of hope

'And surely I am with you always, to the very end of the age.'

It made me jump! Walking past a hedge, I'd been accosted by a cacophony of squawky chirruping – the loudest I'd ever heard – but without a bird in sight. It was as if the shrubbery were alive as they sang their joyful chorus in wild harmony – unseen but most definitely there. I've come across these flocks of hidden chatterbox birds before, but this was a particularly garrulous gathering, squeaking and crackling like a faulty radio.

We don't always need to see things to know they are there. When we cannot be with someone in person for whatever reason, their voice can still remain strong in our lives, surprising us with joy. When Jesus left his disciples, he promised he would always be with them. They could no longer see him but, like those vivacious birds, his voice and presence was – still is – very much there.

Through his time on earth Jesus showed a way of love and truth. Now he gives us his presence and his Spirit to continue that work. And just as the hidden birds made a mightier noise than any I'd ever heard, it was when Jesus physically left the disciples that they received a more powerful outpouring of his presence than they'd ever known before.

■ PRAYER

Thank you, Jesus, for your voice that guides us with joy, reminding us that you will never leave us. Amen

Questions Jesus asked

David Butterfield

Some years ago I was struck by the number of times Jesus asked people questions. So I decided to read through the four gospels over a period of time and write down all the questions he asked in four exercise books, adding comments that occurred to me at the time.

The number of questions Jesus asks is quite striking. In the four gospels he asked about 300 questions. Some are single questions and others are in clusters when he asks a number of questions one after the other. Some are 'closed' questions that only require a one-word answer. But most of them are 'open' questions that challenge his hearers to think about what he asked.

In these reflections, I have chosen ten very different questions that Jesus asked and have added comments about each one. Questions can penetrate our minds much more than statements do. As you reflect on these questions, I hope you might gain a deeper insight into them. And in the future, when you hear a passage from the gospels being read, or read it for yourself, you might like to look out for the questions that Jesus asked and consider how you might answer them.

Luke 10:36 (NIV)

The good Samaritan

'Which of these three do you think was a neighbour to the man who fell into the hands of robbers?'

Jesus told this very well-known parable in response to the question, 'Who is my neighbour?' You will probably recall that it's about a man, travelling down from Jerusalem to Jericho, who was attacked by robbers who left him half dead. A priest and then a Levite came along, but both passed by on the other side.

A Samaritan then came along. When he saw the man lying in the road, Jesus said that his heart was filled with pity. This was extraordinary because there was great animosity and hatred between Jews and Samaritans.

The Samaritan tended the man's wounds and took him to an inn and paid the innkeeper to look after him. It is clear, therefore, that it was the Samaritan who turned out to be a neighbour to the man who had been attacked and robbed. So I think Jesus was saying that anyone we come across in life who we can help is our neighbour, whoever that person may be.

Might there be someone you know to whom you could be a neighbour? It could be someone you don't like very much. Could you think of something positive to say to that person that would bless them?

■ **PRAYER**

Lord Jesus, please bring someone to my mind who I could bless with kind words or with a gift today. Amen

Luke 17:17–18 (NIV)

Where are the other nine?

Jesus asked, 'Were not all ten cleansed? Where are the other nine? Has no one returned to give praise to God except this foreigner?'

When our children were small, we taught them to say 'thank you' when they received Christmas and birthday presents. It's a good habit to acquire.

One day, when Jesus was travelling to Jerusalem, he was met by ten men who had leprosy. Because leprosy is highly contagious, they were not allowed to go near people. So they stood at a distance and called out to Jesus in a loud voice, 'Jesus, Master, have pity on us!'

Jesus said, 'Go, show yourselves to the priests.' In those days the priests were the nearest thing to medical officers. As they went, they were all healed from their leprosy. Only one of them thought to go back and say 'thank you' to Jesus, which is why Jesus asked the three questions.

Even when life is tough, there are many things for which we can be thankful. You could write a list of the things you are thankful for today, and then, like the man healed from leprosy, you could praise God for each one.

■ PRAYER

Heavenly Father, give me a thankful heart. Help me to remember to praise you every day for your blessings. Amen

Matthew 27:46 (NIV)

When God feels distant

About three in the afternoon Jesus cried out in a loud voice, '*Eli, Eli, lema sabachthani*?' (which means 'My God, my God, why have you forsaken me?').

Over the years that I served as a Church of England clergyman, there were many occasions when I visited people who were going through tough times. On some of those occasions people told me that they felt that God had deserted them. It can be devastating when a Christian feels abandoned by God.

When he was dying on the cross, Jesus asked God the question: 'My God, my God, why have you forsaken me?' We cannot begin to comprehend what it must have been like to suffer both the physical pain of crucifixion and the spiritual pain of feeling abandoned by God. If there are times when you feel that God is far away, it would be helpful to recall that Jesus knows what it feels like, and that he is there to help you.

In the poem 'Footprints',* the writer notices that during the saddest and most troublesome times of her life there was only one set of footprints in the sand and assumed that Jesus had deserted her. So she questions Jesus about this. The poem ends with Jesus saying, 'When you saw only one set of footprints, it was then that I carried you.'

■ PRAYER

Thank you, Lord Jesus, that you have said, 'I will never leave you or forsake you' (Hebrews 13:5, NRSV). Help me to hold on to this through the difficult times as well as in the easier times of life. Amen

*The poem 'Footprints' was written by Margaret Fishback Powers in 1964 when she was a young woman searching for direction at a crossroads in her life.

Mark 4:13 (NIV)

Eyes to see

Jesus said to [his disciples], 'Don't you understand this parable? How then will you understand any parable?'

Jesus asked these two questions just after he had told the parable of the sower to a crowd of people by the Sea of Galilee. You may recall that, in the parable, some of the seed fell on the path, some on rocky places, some among thorns and some among good soil. In asking these questions it would seem that Jesus realised that his disciples had not understood what he had been teaching them.

I have never been able to fathom why it is that some people who hear the good news of Jesus immediately understand it and respond positively to what they have heard, whereas others just don't get it. The parable of the sower challenges us to examine our hearts and ask ourselves the question: 'Is my heart like the path, the rocky places, the thorns or the good soil?'

One way we can respond to this challenge is by using the prayer below that Paul included in his letter to Christians in Ephesus (Ephesians 1:18).

■ PRAYER

Heavenly Father, I pray that the eyes of my heart may be enlightened. Amen

Mark 13:1–2 (NIV)

The glory of church buildings

As Jesus was leaving the temple, one of his disciples said to him, 'Look, Teacher! What massive stones! What magnificent buildings!' 'Do you see all these great buildings?' replied Jesus. 'Not one stone here will be left on another; every one will be thrown down.'

From 2014 to 2017 I served for a quarter of my time as a Residentiary Canon of York Minster. Before then I had never envisaged serving in a cathedral. However, as a Yorkshireman I have always regarded York Minster as the grandest cathedral in England!

While I was there, I learned a lot about the building and, during services, would often look up and marvel at its stunning architecture. Jesus' disciples were also awe-struck by the magnificence of the temple in Jerusalem. It must have been a great shock when Jesus foretold its destruction.

Many church buildings have a special place in people's hearts, particularly with memories of family weddings and Christmas carol services and other grand occasions. But there is a danger that we are taken by the splendour of the building rather than the splendour of God. So while we thank God for beautiful church buildings, we need always to keep in mind that they are there to aid our worship and point us God.

■ **PRAYER**
Think of a church building that has a special place in your heart. Pray for those who worship there that the building will point them to the glory of God.

Matthew 7:3–4 (NRSV)

A speck and a log

'Why do you see the speck in your neighbour's eye but do not notice the log in your own eye? Or how can you say to your neighbour, "Let me take the speck out of your eye", while the log is in your own eye?'

I wonder if, like me, you easily spot other people's bad habits. It could be friends or family members. I think my wife and I could easily come up with a list of one another's shortcomings! It's a fact of life that we can be so quick to spot the foibles of others while not noticing our own.

Today's question is part of the sermon on the mount. We can imagine his original hearers laughing, as Jesus painted a picture of a person with a log in his eye. But surely the laughter faded when he went on to say that we should first take the log out of our own eye before we can even think about helping our neighbours with the specks they have in their eyes.

One antidote to noticing the 'logs' in people's eyes is actively to look for the good qualities that a person has. We could think of someone we know and list half-a-dozen positive aspects of that person's character, and then turn it into a prayer, thanking God for that person.

■ PRAYER

Heavenly Father, help me not to focus on the irritating habits of others, but instead to look for the good in people and to thank you for them. Amen

Matthew 6:26–27 (NIV)

Do not worry

'Look at the birds of the air; they do not sow or reap or store away in barns, and yet your heavenly Father feeds them. Are you not much more valuable than they? Can any one of you by worrying add a single hour to your life?'

You may have heard of John Stott, who was a well-known Bible teacher and author. From his childhood he was an enthusiastic bird-watcher. Aware that some people might regard ornithology to be a somewhat eccentric pastime, in one of his books he points out that bird-watching was a command of Jesus.

'Look at the birds of the air,' says Jesus, pointing out how God our heavenly Father feeds them. Then comes the question, 'Are you not much more valuable than they?'

In saying this Jesus was teaching us not to worry, and in a second question he reminds us that worrying does no good. Yet, not worrying is easier said than done. There can be so many things to worry about.

Jesus' antidote to worry is deliberately to put our trust in our heavenly Father. As we read in Psalm 55:22, 'Cast your burden upon the Lord and he will sustain you; he will never allow the righteous to be shaken' (NASB). So next time you find yourself worrying about something, why not turn it into a prayer?

■ PRAYER

Heavenly Father, when worries come my way, help me to cast my burdens on to you. Thank you that you will never allow the righteous to be shaken. Amen

Luke 15:8–10 (NIV)

The lost coin

'Suppose a woman has ten silver coins and loses one. Doesn't she light a lamp, sweep the house and search carefully until she finds it? When she finds it, she calls her friends and neighbours and says, "Rejoice with me; I have found my lost coin." In the same way, I tell you, there is rejoicing in the presence of the angels of God over one sinner who repents.'

When I was in my teens I had a morning paper round. One Saturday, having been paid £1 for my week's work, I cycled four miles into Bradford to buy some piano music. When I got there, I discovered that the £1 note had dropped out of my pocket. I felt so frustrated.

It can be really infuriating to lose something, especially if it is valuable. We might retrace our steps as we search for it, but often with no success. The climax of Jesus' story is the sheer joy the woman feels when she finds her lost coin. The point of the parable is to help us to realise the joy that is felt in heaven when we turn away from sin.

So is there some thought, word or deed that you and I may need to confess to God? If we do this, the parable assures us that there will be a party in heaven.

■ PRAYER

Heavenly Father, may the thought of angels rejoicing in heaven encourage me to ask your forgiveness for anything that I know is wrong in my life. Amen

John 20:29 (RSV)

Doubting Thomas

Jesus said to [Thomas], 'Have you believed because you have seen me? Blessed are those who have not seen and yet believe.'

On the evening of the first Easter Day, Jesus appeared to his disciples. It must have been an amazing experience for them. As you probably know, Thomas was not present on that momentous occasion and he refused to believe that Jesus had risen from the dead.

A week later, Jesus appeared again to his disciples and, this time, Thomas was there. Jesus invited him to touch his wounds and to stop doubting and to believe. Thomas responded by saying, 'My Lord and my God!'

It's at this point that Jesus asks him the question, 'Have you believed because you have seen me?' He follows the question with a statement that speaks to you and me today: 'Blessed are those who have not seen and yet believe.'

So all these centuries later, if you believe in Jesus without seeing him, you are blessed. I like the word 'blessed'. It's a much deeper word than 'happy' or 'lucky' because it implies that someone is blessing us, and we know that the one blessing us is God himself. So if you believe in Jesus, take it to heart – you are blessed.

■ PRAYER
Lord Jesus Christ, thank you that because I believe in you, I am blessed. May I have a sense of your blessing today and every day. Amen

Luke 24:17, 25–26 (NIV)

The road to Emmaus

'What are you discussing together as you walk along?... How foolish you are, and how slow to believe all that the prophets have spoken! Did not the Messiah have to suffer these things and then enter his glory?'

I have always loved this story of how, on the first Easter Day, two of Jesus' followers set out on a seven-mile walk from Jerusalem to the village of Emmaus. They must have felt dejected after all that had happened in Jerusalem that weekend.

At one point Jesus came along and walked with them, but they were kept from recognising him. Jesus then asked them the question: 'What are you discussing together as you walk along?' He then explained some of the Old Testament prophecies about himself.

Later, at the meal table their eyes were opened. They recognised Jesus but he then disappeared from their sight. They then asked each other, 'Were not our hearts burning within us while he talked with us on the road and opened the scriptures to us?'

Sometimes when we read the scriptures there can be a dullness, such that we don't engage with what we are reading. Yet there can be other times when the Holy Spirit causes our hearts to burn within us. Let's pray for that to be true for us.

■ **PRAYER**

Lord Jesus, when I read the Bible, please reveal its truth to me, so that my heart might burn within me. Amen

A worldwide community of faith

Divided tongues, as of fire, appeared among them, and a tongue rested on each of them. All of them were filled with the Holy Spirit and began to speak in other languages, as the Spirit gave them ability.
ACTS 2:3–4 (NRSV)

This edition covers the period of Ascensiontide and Pentecost, a time for marvelling at the wonder of Christ ascending to heaven and the Spirit being sent down to be with us all, uniting us in Christ, beyond the boundaries of countries and languages.

Our Messy Church team is deep in the reality of this worldwide community of faith with the Messy Church Conference 2025 and Key Leaders Gathering. These events take a huge amount of planning and we are grateful to all who have been involved in making them happen.

The Anna Chaplaincy, Living Faith and Parenting for Faith teams are equally busy with training courses, attending conferences, bringing people together and equipping and resourcing people in their ministries and everyday lives.

None of this would be possible without the faith-filled generosity of our supporters. Regular giving, one-off donations, gifts in wills, grants from charitable trusts, responses to appeals and top-up donations with purchases or event bookings – every single gift helps us provide the resources that touch lives around the world. Thank you.

Find out more at **brf.org.uk/donate** or get in touch with us on **01235 462305** or via **giving@brf.org.uk**.

The fundraising team at BRF Ministries

Using the biblical idea of pilgrimage, Sally Welch walks alongside us as leader and guide, but also fellow traveller, to explore how we can understand this biblical principle and make it our own. This book is divided into sections of a journey, beginning with the preparations necessary before setting out, exploring the obstacles which might be put in our path and sharing ways in which the journey can be made easier and more productive. At the end of each reflection there is a suggestion for an activity or prayer to enable the reader to apply the learning to their own life..

Journey to Contentment
Pilgrimage principles for everday life
Sally Welch
978 0 85746 592 4 £8.99
brfonline.org.uk

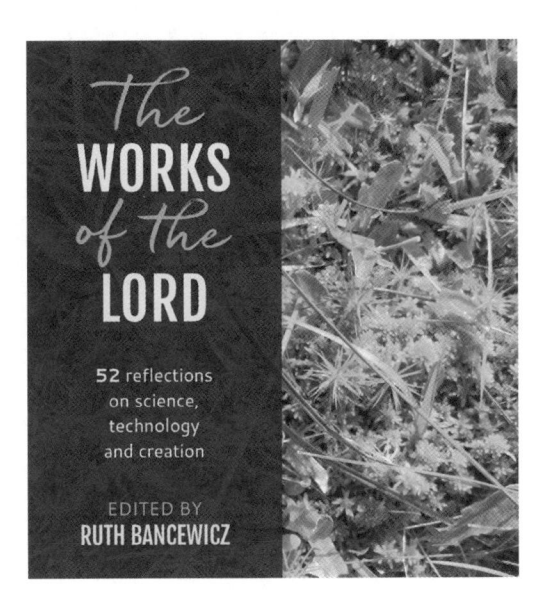

We all benefit from science, and we all make choices about how to use its fruits. This series of reflections lets scientific discoveries fuel your worship and helps you to consider how we can move forward wisely in a scientific society. Written by a diverse group of scientists and theologians associated with the Faraday Institute for Science and Religion in Cambridge, UK, you are invited into the conversation whether you are a scientist or not, and you are given the opportunity to respond in both praise and practical action.

The Works of the Lord
52 reflections on science, technology and creation
Edited by Ruth Bancewicz
978 1 80039 285 4 £14.99
brfonline.org.uk

To order

Online: **brfonline.org.uk**
Telephone: +44 (0)1865 319700
Mon–Fri 9.30–17.00
Post: complete this form and send to the address below

Delivery times within the UK are normally 15 working days. Prices are correct at the time of going to press but may change without prior notice.

BRF

Title	Issue	Price	Qty	Total
Journey to Contentment		£8.99		
The Works of the Lord		£14.99		
Bible Reflections for Older People (single copy)	May–Aug 2025	£5.75		
Bible Reflections for Older People (single copy)	Sep–Dec 2025	£5.75		

POSTAGE AND PACKING CHARGES

Order value	UK	Europe	Rest of world
Under £7.00	£2.00	Available on request	Available on request
£7.00–£29.99	£3.00		
£30.00 and over	FREE		

*Please complete the Gift Aid declaration below

Total value of books	
Donation*	
Postage and packing	
Total for this order	

Please complete in BLOCK CAPITALS

Title .... First name/initials .... Surname ....

Address ....

.... Postcode ....

Acc. No. .... Telephone ....

Email ....

Method of payment

☐ Cheque (made payable to BRF)   ☐ MasterCard / Visa

Card no. ☐☐☐☐ ☐☐☐☐ ☐☐☐☐ ☐☐☐☐

Expires end M M Y Y   Security code ☐☐☐   Last 3 digits on the reverse of the card

BRF Ministries Gift Aid Declaration

In order to Gift Aid your donations, you must tick the box below.

☐ I want to Gift Aid my donation and any donation I make in the future or have made in the past four years to BRF Ministries.

giftaid it

I am a UK taxpayer and understand that if I pay less Income Tax and/or Capital Gains Tax in the current tax year than the amount of Gift Aid claimed on all my donations, it is my responsibility to pay any difference. Please notify BRF Ministries if you want to cancel this declaration, change your name or home address, or no longer pay sufficient tax on your income and/or capital gains.

Please return this form to:
BRF Ministries, 15 The Chambers, Vineyard, Abingdon OX14 3FE | enquiries@brf.org.uk
For terms and cancellation information, please visit brfonline.org.uk/terms.

We will use your personal data to process this order. From time to time we may send you information about the work of BRF Ministries. Please contact us if you wish to discuss your mailing preferences
brf.org.uk/privacy

Registered with FUNDRAISING REGULATOR

BROP0225

BIBLE REFLECTIONS FOR OLDER PEOPLE GROUP SUBSCRIPTION FORM

All our Bible reading notes can be ordered online by visiting **brfonline.org.uk/subscriptions**

The group subscription rate for *Bible Reflections for Older People* will be £17.25 per person until April 2026.

☐ I would like to take out a group subscription for .... *(quantity)* copies.

☐ Please start my order with the September 2025 / January 2026 / May 2026* issue.
(*delete as appropriate*)

Please do not send any money with your order. Send your order to BRF Ministries and we will send you an invoice.

Name and address of the person organising the group subscription:

Title .... First name/initials .... Surname ....

Address ....

.... Postcode ....

Telephone .... Email ....

Church ....

Name and address of the person paying the invoice if the invoice needs to be sent directly to them:

Title .... First name/initials .... Surname ....

Address ....

.... Postcode ....

Telephone .... Email ....

Please return this form to:
BRF Ministries, 15 The Chambers, Vineyard, Abingdon OX14 3FE | **enquiries@brf.org.uk**
For terms and cancellation information, please visit brfonline.org.uk/terms.

Bible Reading Fellowship is a charity (233280) and company limited by guarantee (301324), registered in England and Wales

BIBLE REFLECTIONS FOR OLDER PEOPLE INDIVIDUAL/GIFT SUBSCRIPTION FORM

To order online or set up a recurring subscription,
visit **brfonline.org.uk/bible-reflections-for-older-people**

☐ I would like to take out a subscription (*complete your name and address details only once*)
☐ I would like to give a gift subscription (*please provide both names and addresses*)

Title .... First name/initials .... Surname...

Address...

.... Postcode ....

Telephone .... Email ....

Gift subscription name ....

Gift subscription address ....

.... Postcode ....

Gift message (*20 words max. or include your own gift card*):

....

....

Please send **Bible Reflections for Older People** beginning with the September 2025 / January 2026 / May 2026* issue (**delete as appropriate*):

(*please tick box*)	UK	Europe	Rest of world
Bible Reflections for Older People	☐ £22.80	☐ £30.75	☐ £37.05

Total enclosed £ .... (*cheques should be made payable to 'BRF'*)

Please charge my MasterCard / Visa with £ ....

Card no. ☐☐☐☐ ☐☐☐☐ ☐☐☐☐ ☐☐☐☐

Expires end M M Y Y   Security code ☐☐☐   Last 3 digits on the reverse of the card

We will use your personal data to process this order. From time to time we may send you information about the work of BRF Ministries. Please contact us if you wish to discuss your mailing preferences **brf.org.uk/privacy**.

Please return this form to:
BRF Ministries, 15 The Chambers, Vineyard, Abingdon OX14 3FE | **enquiries@brf.org.uk**
For terms and cancellation information, please visit brfonline.org.uk/terms.

BRF

Bible Reading Fellowship is a charity (233280) and company limited by guarantee (301324), registered in England and Wales